DISCOVER!

EARTH AND SPACE SCIENCE

WATER ON EARTH

Beth Irving

Enslow PUBLISHING

Please visit our website, www.enslow.com. For a free color catalog of all our high-quality books, call toll free 1-800-398-2504 or fax 1-877-980-4454.

Cataloging-in-Publication Data
Names: Irving, Beth.
Title: Water on Earth / Beth Irving.
Description: Buffalo, NY : Enslow Publishing, 2027. | Series: Earth and space science | Includes glossary and index.
Identifiers: ISBN 9781978550384 (pbk.) | ISBN 9781978550391 (library bound) | ISBN 9781978550407 (ebook)
Subjects: LCSH: Water–Juvenile literature. | Water use–Juvenile literature. | Hydrologic cycle–Juvenile literature.
Classification: LCC GB662.3 I785 2027 | DDC 553.7–dc23

Published in 2027 by
Enslow Publishing
2544 Clinton Street
Buffalo, NY 14224

Designer: Claire Vanden Branden
Editor: Noah Riccardi

Photo Credits: Cover, p. 1 Framalicious/Shutterstock.com; p. 5 Marina Grigorivna/Shutterstock.com; p. 6 Kaentian Street/Shutterstock .com; p. 7 Kaiskynet Studios/Shutterstock.com; p. 9 Pung/Shutterstock.com; p. 11 Nach-Noth/Shutterstock.com; p. 13 Pavel Rumlena/Shutterstock.com; p. 14 Photoframe123/Shutterstock.com; p. 15 Stone36/Shutterstock.com; p. 17 Danii D./Shutterstock.com; p. 19 Vladimir Tretyakov/Shutterstock.com; p. 21 Kiwigoneairborne/Shutterstock.com.

Printed in China

CPSIA compliance information: Batch #QS27ENS: For further information contact Enslow Publishing, at 1-800-398-2504.

CONTENTS

BOLDFACE WORDS APPEAR IN THE GLOSSARY.

A WATERY PLANET

Planet Earth has lots of water. Water covers over 70 percent of its surface. It has so much water, people sometimes call it the Blue Planet.

Most of Earth's water is in the oceans. Some water is in lakes and **streams**. Some water is **frozen** as ice and snow.

Some water goes into the ground after rain. This is called groundwater. Many people dig wells to get to groundwater.

The sun heats water on Earth. This makes some of it go into the air. Water in the air is called **water vapor**.

WATER CYCLE

Earth's water doesn't stay in one place. It moves from the ground to the sky. Then it comes back down to the ground.

The water on Earth does this again and again. It has been doing this for a very long time. This is called Earth's water **cycle**.

WATER IN THE AIR

Water in the air is called water vapor. Water vapor is like the steam you see when you boil water. The sun heats up Earth's water and turns it into water vapor.

Water from plants also turns into water vapor. The water vapor rises up into the sky.

RAINFALL

Water vapor in the sky cools down. This turns it back into tiny drops of water. The tiny drops of water group together and form clouds.

The tiny water drops cling to dust in the clouds. The tiny drops come together to form larger drops. The clouds get bigger and darker.

The water drops in clouds become too heavy to stay in the air. Soon, the water drops fall back to Earth. This falling water is rain.

Rain is an important part of the water cycle. It fills Earth's lakes and rivers. Rain fills Earth's oceans, too.

Some rain **seeps** into the earth. This rain becomes groundwater. Plants need this water to grow. Lots of people use groundwater for drinking and washing.

Sometimes the ground can't hold any more water. Then the water flows downhill over the land. This water forms rivers and streams.

SNOW

When it's cold, rain freezes in clouds. When it falls, this frozen rain is snow. The snow piles up on the ground and on trees.

The snow **melts** when it gets warmer. This melted snow fills up lakes, rivers, and streams. Some melted snow seeps into the earth and becomes groundwater.

BACK TO THE START

After water goes into rivers, oceans, and the Earth, some of it turns back into water vapor. The water cycle starts again.

The water cycle is important to every kind of life on Earth. Earth's water has been here for a long time. It will be here for a long time to come.

GLOSSARY

cycle: Something that happens over and over again.

frozen: Changed from water to ice.

melts: Changes from ice to water.

planet: A large, round object that moves around the sun.

seeps: Passes slowly into or through something.

streams: Small rivers.

water vapor: Water in the form of a gas.

FOR MORE INFORMATION

Books

Chapman, Amy. *The Water Cycle*. Buffalo, NY: Rosen Publishing, 2026.

Schaefer, Lola. *Dangerous Droughts*. Minneapolis, MN: Lerner Publications, 2022.

Websites

Britannica Kids: Water Cycle
kids.britannica.com/kids/article/water-cycle/476333
Learn more about the water cycle here.

PBS LearningMedia: Water Cycle Animation
thinktv.pbslearningmedia.org/resource/ess05.sci.ess.watcyc.watercycle/water-cycle-animation/
Watch how the water cycle happens at this site.

Publisher's note to educators and parents: Our editors have carefully reviewed these websites to ensure that they are suitable for students. Many websites change frequently, however, and we cannot guarantee that a site's future contents will continue to meet our high standards of quality and educational value. Be advised that students should be closely supervised whenever they access the internet.

INDEX